the

simple joys

for

Teachers

Heartwarming Stories & Inspiration to Celebrate Teachers

Ellie Claire
gift & paper expressions

...inspired by life

Ellie Claire® Gift & Paper Corp.
Brentwood, TN 37027
EllieClaire.com
A Worthy Publishing Company

The Simple Joys for Teachers
© 2013 Ellie Claire® Gift & Paper Corp.

ISBN 978-1-60936-809-8

Stock or custom editions of Ellie Claire titles may be purchased in bulk for educational, business, ministry, fundraising, or sales promotional use. For information, please e-mail info@EllieClaire.com.

Compiled by Barbara Farmer
Cover and interior design by ThinkPen | thinkpendesign.com
Illustrations by Julie Sawyer Phillips
Typesetting by Rebekah Mathis

Printed in China
1 2 3 4 5 6 7 8 9 – 18 17 16 15 14 13

Contents

Introduction	There Is No Greater Joy	1
Chapter 1	The Simple Joy of Gratitude	3
Chapter 2	The Simple Joy of Wisdom	17
Chapter 3	The Simple Joy of Kindness	31
Chapter 4	The Simple Joy of Imagination	45
Chapter 5	The Simple Joy of Encouragement	57
Chapter 6	The Simple Joy of Leading	71
Chapter 7	The Simple Joy of Inspiration	85
Chapter 8	The Simple Joy of Humor	97
Chapter 9	The Simple Joy of Sharing	111
Chapter 10	The Simple Joy of Faith	125

Recipes

Edible Candy Mosaic	12
The Sweet Taste of Kindness—Sugar Crystals	36
The Simple Joy of Chocolate!	74

*There is no greater
joy nor greater reward than
to make a fundamental
difference in someone's life.*

MARY ROSE MCGEADY

There Is No Greater Joy

*I*t seems to be a calling—to teach and nurture young minds. What else can it be? No other paid occupation demands as much or delivers so great a return. It is kin to parenting, both having great love at their center.

What are the rewards that come back to each dedicated teacher? They are for the most part simple joys—receiving a special drawing from a timid hand, calming a rug full of wiggly arms and legs with a "Once upon a time…" story, spying the triumphant smile of a student conquering a tricky algebra problem, witnessing the elation of a student sharing knowledge with others.

Our prayer is that *The Simple Joys of Teaching* will inspire you in your daily classroom adventure. We want to encourage you in your creativity, enthusiasm, dedication, and overall excitement as you cultivate the minds of the next generation, leading them into a promising future. For a teacher, there is no greater joy.

~The Editors

CHAPTER 1

The simple joy of Gratitude

Lord, thank You for my students and for sending
these specific ones to me. Please inspire me with ways to show
them my love and Yours. I want them to feel appreciated.
I want to help and encourage them. And I want to bless them
for they have been such a blessing to me.
Amen.

*Let your roots grow down into him, and
let your lives be built on him. Then your faith
will grow strong in the truth you were taught,
and you will overflow with thankfulness.*

COLOSSIANS 2:7 NLT

Bumper Sticker

BY RICK HAMLIN

I thank my God upon every remembrance of you.

PHILIPPIANS 1:3 NKJV

I'm often driven along a highway behind a bumper sticker that states, "If you can read this, you're too close." That's why I was amused the other day to find myself behind one that said, "If you can read this, thank a teacher."

My amusement wavered because I began to think of the lean, white-haired teacher who did teach me to read. Then I recalled, among others, the ones who'd taught me to solve problems, tell time, use a typewriter, translate Spanish, and love Shakespeare. I couldn't remember thanking any of them.

I thought of how much richer my life was because of those teachers, and right there in the car I thanked God for each one.

Gratitude bestows reverence,
allowing us to encounter everyday epiphanies,
those transcendent moments of awe that
change forever how we experience life and the world.

JOHN MILTON

May you experience the love of Christ,
though it is too great to understand fully.
Then you will be made complete with all the
fullness of life and power that comes from God.

EPHESIANS 3:19 NLT

Returning the Favor

BY NANCY B. GIBBS

Give, and it will be given to you. A good measure, pressed down, shaken together and running over, will be poured into your lap. For with the measure you use, it will be measured to you.

LUKE 6:38 NIV

My husband, Roy, put his heart and soul into teaching his eighth-grade classes in a Macon, Georgia, public school. "I'm here for two reasons," he would begin his traditional speech on the first day of every school year. "First of all, I want to prepare you for a bright future and teach you to be the best you can be." Then he would jokingly add, "And second, one day, maybe one of you will take care of me."

Teaching was his life. Roy stayed after school to coach sports, gave extra help to students, and chaperoned field trips. Then one summer afternoon Roy said he didn't feel well. Soon he complained of chest pains and difficulty breathing. I rushed him to a hospital and he ended up having an angioplasty.

Roy was getting some rest afterward when we heard a knock on his hospital room door. A young nurse popped her head in. "Mr. Gibbs," she said, "I guess I'm the one." Puzzled, Roy asked, "What do you mean?" The nurse explained, "You were my favorite teacher in eighth grade. On the first day of class you gave a speech I never forgot. Now I plan to take very good care of you."

Thank you for your laughter, warm smile, and
ever-present love that so often lifts me up
above the clouds to where the sun is always shining.

*Pray diligently. Stay alert, with your
eyes wide open in gratitude.*

COLOSSIANS 4:2 MSG

Thank you for believing in me
before I believed in myself.

THE ATTITUDE OF GRATITUDE

Six fun ways to show your students how thankfulness can be rewarding.

1. Listen and Learn: Ask your students to keep track of the sounds they are thankful for. Make a top ten list for each student and then one for the classroom.

2. Count Your Blessings: Let students make individual or collective collages to display all the things for which they are grateful.

3. Appreciation Station: When there's a disruptive complainer or a grumpy student in the class, let them take a time out where they can focus on some positive input. Decorate the station with inspiring quotes and pictures, stock it with art supplies and inspiring books, and offer headphones to let them listen to music that uplifts. Let them see you use it once in a while.

4. "Thank You" Toss: Gather in a circle and with a beanbag or other soft item begin a game of catch where the person tossing the ball has to say one thing they are thankful for.

5. Share the Love: Offer the students an opportunity to bless other people. Make gifts or cards for soldiers or the elderly, collect items for a food shelf, or donate their gently used toys to Good Will or the Salvation Army.

6. Time Capsule: Put together a tin box or coffee can filled with notes or items that share with the next generation what students are most thankful for.

Thank You, God, for little things
That often come our way,
The things we take for granted
But don't mention when we pray.

The unexpected courtesy,
The thoughtful kindly deed,
A hand reached out to help us
In the time of sudden need.

Oh, make us more aware, dear God,
Of little daily graces
That come to us with sweet surprise
From never-dreamed-of places.

Whatever you do in word or deed, do all in the name of the Lord Jesus,
giving thanks to God the Father through Him.

COLOSSIANS 3:17 NKJV

Common Denominator

BY Z. B. D.

Love is patient, love is kind....
It always protects, always trusts, always hopes,
always perseveres. Love never fails.

1 CORINTHIANS 13:4, 7–8 NIV

*S*everal years ago a young professor at Johns Hopkins University gave members of his sociology class an unusual assignment. "Go into the worst slums of Baltimore," he told them. "Find and interview 200 boys; study their backgrounds, their surroundings, their opportunities—and predict their future."

In searching out the 200 boys, the students were appalled by the housing, the environment, the broken homes, the alcoholism, the delinquency, the lack of inspiration, and the absence of example. They predicted that 180 of the 200 boys would serve time in prison.

Twenty-five years passed. The same professor assigned another class the task of finding the 200 boys and reporting on the outcome of the prediction. They were able to find most of the original boys— but the opposite of the prediction was true; they were fine citizens. Only four had been in jail.

The next assignment was to find some common denominator in the lives of the boys that brought this about. They found it in a high school teacher, Sheila O'Rourke. Many of the boys told of Miss O'Rourke having been an inspiration in their lives. "She cared," was their summation.

Miss O'Rourke, then seventy and living in a nursing home, was told of the survey made, the predictions, the outcome of the predictions, and of her influence in their lives. Asked to comment she answered, "All I can say is that I loved every one of them."

God, grant me wisdom,
Grant me vision,
Grant me courage,
Grant me love,
To teach a child.

IDA NELLE HOLLAWAY

EDIBLE CANDY MOSAIC

Enjoy this sweet treat with your students. A great way to show thanks to them or to help them say thanks to someone else. Perfect for many different holidays and celebrations.

You will need:
- Jellybeans, M&Ms®, Skittles®, or other colorful round candies
- Frosting (homemade or pre-packaged) for "glue"
- Various cookie cutters to press design shapes in frosting
- Graham crackers for "canvas"

Directions:
Spread frosting onto graham crackers. Use a cookie cutter to imprint an occasion-specific design into frosting and fill it in with candy. Or make freestyle designs with cookie cutters and/or candies.

The joy of receiving is in far more than the gifts—
that when we receive graciously and gladly,
we reciprocate the gift with joy and gratitude; and in
that moment of shared happiness and understanding,
giver and receiver "connect."

JENNY WALTON

Gratitude unlocks the fullness of life.
It turns what we have into enough, and more....
It turns problems into gifts, failures into
successes, the unexpected into perfect timing,
and mistakes into important events.

MELODY BEATTIE

You make known to me the path of life;
you will fill me with joy in your presence,
with eternal pleasures at your right hand.

PSALM 16:11 NIV

HOW DO YOU SAY THANK YOU TO A TEACHER?

- Alphabetically and/or numerically is a great way to start.
- As grammatically correct as possible.
- With proper punctuation.
- Using as many descriptive words that can apply.
- Being careful not to dangle any participles.
- Choosing an active voice, not passive.
- An added thoughtful interjection is always nice.
- Run-on sentences are okay if they include a list of all the teacher's positive attributes.
- No fragmented sentences, please.
- At least a full paragraph long.
- Don't forget to illustrate—crayon or washable markers are preferred.
- Cutting out and pasting designs is highly recommended but not required.
- Signing your name using the cursive method is a great way to impress.

Basically, thanking a teacher for all they've taught you using all they've taught you is the best thank-you a teacher could get.

*If I were to make a solemn speech
in praise of you, in gratitude, in deep affection,
you would turn an alarming shade of
crimson and try to escape.
So I won't. Take it all as said.*

MARION C. GARRETTY

We always thank God for all of you and continually mention you in our prayers. We remember before our God and Father your work produced by faith, your labor prompted by love, and your endurance inspired by hope in our Lord Jesus Christ.

1 THESSALONIANS 1:2–3 NIV

Honor Roll

Teachers affect eternity;
they can never tell
where their influence stops.

HENRY BROOKS ADAMS

CHAPTER 2

The simple joy of Wisdom

A child's hand in yours—what tenderness and power it arouses.
You are instantly the very touchstone of wisdom and strength.

MARJORIE HOLMES

Wisdom from above is first of all pure. It is also
peace loving, gentle at all times, and willing to yield to others.
It is full of mercy and good deeds.
It shows no favoritism and is always sincere.

JAMES 3:17 NLT

Teacher Defined

FROM DICTIONARY © 2005–2011 APPLE INC.

teach |tēCH|

verb (past and past participle **taught** |tôt|) [with obj. and infinitive or clause]
show or explain to (someone) how to do something:
she taught him to read | *he taught me how to ride a bike.*
• [with obj.] give information about or instruction in (a subject
or skill):
he came one day each week to teach painting | [with two objs.] : *she teaches
me French.*
• [no obj.] give such instruction professionally:
she teaches at the local high school.
• [with obj.] encourage someone to accept (something) as a
fact or principle: *the philosophy teaches self-control.*
• cause (someone) to learn or understand something by example
or experience: *she'd been taught that it paid to be passive* | *my upbringing
taught me never to be disrespectful to elders.*

teacher |tēCHər|

noun
a person who teaches, esp. in a school.

teach synonyms

verb

1 *Alison teaches small children*:
educate, instruct, school, tutor, coach, train;
enlighten, illuminate, edify, discipline.

2 *I taught yoga*:
give lessons in, be a teacher of; demonstrate, instill.

3 *She taught me how to love*:
train, show, guide, instruct, explain to, demonstrate to.

teacher

noun

1 *the new teacher makes math fun*:
educator, tutor, instructor, master, mistress, governess,
educationist, preceptor; coach, trainer; lecturer, professor,
don; guide, mentor, guru, counselor.

Instruct the wise and they will be wiser still;
teach the righteous and they will add to their learning.

PROVERBS 9:9 NIV

Beauty for Ashes

BY WINIFRED WALTNER

To all who mourn...he will give a crown of beauty for ashes,
a joyous blessing instead of mourning.

ISAIAH 61:3 NLT

When I was an American teenager growing up in China, I was intrigued by Oriental brush painting. I studied the ancient art and learned to paint with a bamboo brush. The artist must be disciplined, precise, and supremely self-assured. You can't erase your mistakes from rice paper. In the United States in 1972, I began to teach courses in the art. But I found I had one more lesson to learn.

It was the last day of class. The students prepared their supplies to paint a traditional garden scene. I had promised to bring in one of my own paintings of bamboo. A murmur of approval rippled through the class as I carefully unrolled the scroll. My masterpiece, I thought as I hung it near my desk. Here was my example of all I had been trying to teach my students.

We began to paint on new sheets of rice paper. I wanted a lighter shade, so I washed my brush a few times and flicked it to remove the excess water. Then I heard a collective gasp. All eyes were on my displayed painting. Spots of gray ink had splattered on the scroll when I flicked my brush. I had ruined my masterpiece! You can't erase on rice paper. My face reddened. *Some expert teacher*, I thought. *Lord, show me what to do.*

Then I got an idea. With my brush I painted in four more dots along with each gray dot, making a plum blossom out of each. With a few light touches I added sepals and pollen dots, then twigs, so that a complete branch of plum intertwined with the bamboo. When I finished, the students burst into applause.

I still remember the lesson I learned that day. We can't erase our mistakes, but when we ask God to take control, we can be shown how to find beauty in our errors.

TWELVE THINGS TO REMEMBER

FROM MARSHALL FIELD

1. The value of time.
2. The success of perseverance.
3. The pleasure of working.
4. The dignity of simplicity.
5. The worth of character.
6. The power of kindness.
7. The influence of example.
8. The obligation of duty.
9. The wisdom of economy.
10. The virtue of patience.
11. The improvement of talent.
12. The joy of origination.

Teach us to number our days,
that we may gain a heart of wisdom.

PSALM 90:12 NIV

*The fairest flower in the garden of creation
is a young mind, offering and unfolding itself
to the influence of divine wisdom.*

J. E. SMITH

Life is not about discovering our talents;
it is about pushing our talents
to the limit and discovering our genius.

ROBERT BRAULT

Learning sleeps and snores in libraries,
but wisdom is everywhere, wide awake, on tiptoe.

JOSH BILLINGS

Lesson Learned

BY B. W. D.

Students are not greater than their teacher. But the student
who is fully trained will become like the teacher.

LUKE 6:40 NLT

*O*ne day during the second year of my teaching career I abruptly slammed shut the book I'd been reading to my class, an unruly bunch of eleventh-grade boys who'd been driving me to distraction with their rude talking.

"That's all," I announced. "I refuse to teach you."

Baiting me, one of the boys said, "You can't refuse. You have to teach us. It's your job."

"Wrong," I snapped. "If I am to be a teacher, then you must be *students*. From now on, I will teach only my *students*."

To my amazement, I had finally made an impression on them. Little by little, every boy in the class asked to join the "student" section.

Years later, during a particularly frustrating period in my life, I was crying out to God, *"You have to help me, God. I'm in trouble. Where are You?"*

Suddenly, my mouth closed and my ears opened. My arrogant intellect sat down in its seat. With a healing rush of humility, it occurred to me to ask permission to join His "student" section.

And what a teacher He is!

The instruction of the wise is like a life-giving fountain.

PROVERBS 13:14 NLT

24

We learn wisdom from failure much more than from success. We often discover what will do by finding out what will not do; and probably he who never made a mistake never made a discovery.

SAMUEL SMILES

Wisdom is the power to see, and the inclination to choose, the best and highest goal, together with the surest means of attaining it.

J. I. PACKER

Give me a fruitful error any time, full of seeds, bursting with its own corrections.

VILFREDO PARETO

Finding Wisdom

BY MARILYN MORGAN KING

Blessed are those who find wisdom,
those who gain understanding.

PROVERBS 3:13 NIV

*D*ear Tiny Toes,
As I look deep into your eyes, I wonder what you see and hear. Even now, you are learning by fully living in every moment.

This winding path of discovery will continue for as long as you live. You will find that the knowledge that comes from books and study will greatly enrich your life; always seek for ever deeper answers to the questions that will surely arise out of your own curiosity. May you also discover that some questions can't be answered, no matter how hard you try. Try anyway, and keep on trying.

I hope you will hold on to some questions whose answers elude you. You see, there's a hidden treasure far greater than pinned-down truths—wisdom. Wisdom won't announce itself. You'll find it in the secrets of trees that whisper in the silence and of clouds that speak in pictures. You'll find it in church when the words you sing swell your heart, as well as on the playground when the teacher calls "Foul!" and you're suddenly full of shame. Wisdom comes from holding on to questions. Just be still and gradually you will come to know deeper questions that will lead you beyond yourself. You will know the territory by the throbbing of your heart.

Wisdom from God shows itself most clearly in a loving heart.

LLOYD JOHN OGILVIE

How to Punctuate Life

BY SUE MONK KIDD

Incline your ear unto wisdom,
and apply your heart to understanding.

PROVERBS 2:2 NKJV

Rules of punctuation for the "real world."

1. A question mark is your best tool for prying open new horizons. Keep a "Great Questions" notebook. Every great discovery begins with a great question, like: "How can I make a difference in the world?"

2. Mark your declarations firmly with a period. Search your mind and heart for what you believe, then have the courage to declare it, period.

3. Use commas to create pauses in your day. You need time to reflect, dream, listen, pray, and nourish the soul. Without such pauses, life gets confused and garbled.

4. Bend as many moments as you can into exclamation points. In God's glorious world, the greatest way to appreciate life is to live it with passion, wonder, and emphasis!

Right now I think I'll take a long pause (,) and recline in the warm green shadows in my backyard. While there I may just ask myself some provocative questions (?). Or maybe I'll come to terms with how I really feel (.) about some issues I've been waffling on lately. And as the wonder of the spring day spills through me, I suspect the word that comes to my lips will be "Wow!"(!)

Honor Roll

He that teaches us
anything which we knew not before
is undoubtedly to be
reverenced as a master.

SAMUEL JOHNSON

CHAPTER 3

The simple joy of Kindness

Kind words can be short
and easy to speak, but
their echoes are truly endless.

MOTHER TERESA

She opens her mouth in wisdom,
And the teaching of kindness is on her tongue.

PROVERBS 31:26 NASB

Ain't Misbehavin'

BY CATHERINE SCOTT

In kindness he takes us firmly by the hand
and leads us into a radical life-change.

ROMANS 2:4 MSG

*S*chool counselor Piet Lammert was looking for new ways to inspire the students at East Belfast School in Maine when he heard about a program in which kids agree to perform good deeds and log them in a journal.

Piet had a perfect test case in mind: a class of 20 fifth graders who had a reputation for out-of-control behavior. "They weren't bad kids, just unfocused," Piet says. "We wanted to give them some direction before they went on to middle school." He set a goal of 33 good deeds per student, totaling 660 acts of kindness altogether over the year.

The kids took to the idea with surprising enthusiasm and, one by one, the deeds piled up: visiting a nursing home, organizing a penny drive for the local animal shelter, shoveling snow for a neighbor, taking notes for sick classmates, rescuing stray cats during a storm. Every day the kids traded stories of their latest acts of charity, and the class bonded in a way neither Piet nor their teacher, Trudy Eldridge, had ever seen before.

The class reached its mark of 660 deeds before the end of the school year—and kept on going. "We lost track after seven hundred and fifty," says Piet. "And a few kids have started their third journal already." Nowadays it isn't the kids but the kindness that's out of control at East Belfast!

The best way to ensure that your children grow to become kind and compassionate adults is to teach them how to be kind and compassionate children.

KATHRYN SANSONE

Those who make compassion an essential
part of their lives find the joy of life.
Kindness deepens the spirit and produces rewards
that cannot be completely explained in words.
It is an experience more powerful than words.
To become acquainted with kindness
one must be prepared to learn new things and
feel new feelings. Kindness is more than
a philosophy of the mind.
It is a philosophy of the spirit.

ROBERT J. FUREY

Never let loyalty and kindness leave you!
Tie them around your neck as a reminder.
Write them deep within your heart.
Then you will find favor with both God and people,
and you will earn a good reputation.

PROVERBS 3:3–4 NLT

THE SWEET TASTE OF KINDNESS CRYSTALS

This is a sweet project for kids of most any age.

You will need:
- 6 cups sugar
- 2 cups water
- Food coloring (four different colors)
- 4 half pint jars
- 4 popsicle sticks or pencils
- rough string or yarn (not smooth)

Heat water in a saucepan until boiling. Add sugar slowly until it will no longer dissolve. Let the solution cool for ten minutes. Pour sugar water into jars, dividing evenly between all four. Add a few drops of food coloring to each jar, giving each a unique color.

Tie a piece of string or yarn securely to the stick/pencil, cutting the string to be three-fourths the depth of the jar. Place the string into the middle of the jar and rest the stick on the top. The string should not touch the bottom of the jar.

Cover the top of the jar with a paper towel or tissue paper. Let set for about four days. The water in your bowls will evaporate little by little each day and leave sugar crystals behind.

Our sweetest experiences
of affection are meant to point us
to that realm which is the real
and endless home of the heart.

HENRY WARD BEECHER

Mighty Little Note

BY ADRIAN DEGALAN

Clothe yourselves with compassion, kindness, humility, gentleness and patience.

COLOSSIANS 3:12 NIV

When I was a first-year teacher, Debbie was one of my favorite students. No one could resist her; she was cute as a button with her curly brown hair and big brown eyes. Deb had a way of melting your heart.

My second year was to be spent with a large class, squeezed into a tiny, old basement classroom. It was a bit discouraging to see all the desks crammed close together with little room to pass among the students.

A few days after the start of school I opened my desk to take attendance one morning. I found a small, white piece of paper in the desk drawer. On it was written: "I know forty very lucky kids!" It was signed Debbie.

I can't tell you how good it made me feel. I will always remember that as the most pleasant beginning to a school year that I have ever had. My sagging morale was sent soaring by a kind note from a loving eleven-year-old girl.

Listening...means taking a vigorous, human interest
in what is being told us. You can listen like
a blank wall or like a splendid auditorium where
every sound comes back fuller and richer.

ALICE DUER MILLER

*The nicest thing we can do for our heavenly
Father is to be kind to one of His children.*

TERESA OF AVILA

Be kind and compassionate to one another.

EPHESIANS 4:32 NIV

I expect to pass through life but once. If, therefore, there can be any
kindness I can show, or any good thing I can do to any
fellow being, let me do it now...as I shall not pass this way again.

STEPHEN GRELLET

When There Is a Need

BY ALMA HENDRIX MCNATT

Heavenly Father,

When there is a need for teaching, teach through me.

When there is need for a message, speak through me.

When there is a need for love, love through me.

When there is a need for music, sing through me.

When there is a need for understanding, listen through me.

When there is need for counseling, advise through me.

When a gift is needed, give through me.

Whenever prayer is needed, pray through me.

When a helping hand is needed, reach through mine.

God sends children to enlarge our hearts and to make us
unselfish and full of kindly sympathies and affections.

MARY HOWITT

If your gift is serving others, serve them well.
If you are a teacher, teach well.
If your gift is to encourage others, be encouraging....
And if you have a gift for showing kindness
to others, do it gladly.

ROMANS 12:7–8 NLT

*They may forget what you said, but they
will never forget how you made them feel.*

CARL W. BUECHNER

A Genius for Loving

BY MARY ANN BIRD

Don't just pretend to love others. Really love them.
ROMANS 12:9 NLT

I was born with a cleft palate, and my classmates made it clear to me how I must look to others: a little girl with a misshapen lip, crooked nose, lopsided teeth, and somewhat garbled speech. By the age of seven I was convinced that no one outside my own family could ever love me.

And then I entered second grade and Mrs. Leonard's class. She had warm, dark eyes that smiled even when her mouth didn't. Everyone adored her. But no one more than I did.

The time came for the annual hearing tests given at our school. I was barely able to hear anything out of one ear, and was not about to reveal yet another problem that would single me out as different. So I cheated.

I had learned to watch the other children and raise my hand when they did during group testing. The "whisper test," however, required a different kind of deception: Each child would go to the door of the classroom, turn sideways, close one ear with a finger, and the teacher would whisper something from her desk, which the child would repeat. Then the same thing was done for the other ear. Nobody checked to see how tightly the untested ear was being covered, so I pretended to block mine.

All through the testing I wondered what Mrs. Leonard might say to me. My turn came. I pretended to plug my ear and waited, and then came the words that God had surely put into her mouth, words that changed my life forever, "I wish you were my little girl."

We listen to words but hear with our hearts.

Honor Roll

Caring teachers are among
our nation's greatest treasures;
they are entrusted with its future.

CHAPTER 4

The simple joy of Imagination

Whatever you do, put romance and enthusiasm
into the lives of our children.

MARGARET R. MACDONALD

God can do anything, you know—
far more than you could ever imagine or guess
or request in your wildest dreams!

EPHESIANS 3:20 MSG

No More Math Problems

BY C. A.

Make the most of every opportunity.
EPHESIANS 5:16 NLT

I know an elementary teacher who was discouraged about his students' progress in math. "I know they're bright kids because I've seen their aptitude test results," he told me. "But their daily work is disappointing. I'm afraid I'm not bringing out the best in them."

Not long after, this same teacher told his class, "From now on, we'll have no more math problems." The class cheered. "Starting now, we'll have only have math *challenges*."

From then on he always introduced new math concepts in terms of challenging games or puzzles. The word "problem" was banished from his classroom.

At semester's end, each of his students was at grade level or above in his math skills. My friend's secret was substituting a positive word for a negative one. It changed the attitude of the whole class.

Another friend who works in a busy office puts it this way: "I thank God every day for the things that go wrong on my job. If there weren't problems there that require my specific skills and talents, I could be replaced by a computer."

Problems really *are* challenges. The key is in how you look at them.

INCONCEIVABLE!

(AN AMAZING MATH TRICK)

- Divide your students into groups of three.
- Pick a student spokesperson from each group and have him or her choose any number from 1 to 20.
- The students must not disclose the number they have chosen.
- Tell them to multiply the number by 2. Make sure they do the calculations in their head.
- After they have finished, have them add 10 to the answer.
- Then ask them to divide the result by 2.
- Finally, have them take the result and subtract it from the original number they had chosen.
- Watch their awed expression when you announce that the final result for all of them is 5.

Let early education be a sort of amusement; you will then be better able to find out the natural bent.

PLATO

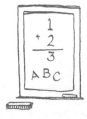

Time Out

BY ELIZABETH SHERRILL

My times are in your hands.

PSALM 31:15 NIV

I discovered the wisdom of "minute vacations" when my husband and I were on an actual vacation. In the Florida panhandle, we had stopped at a restaurant set in a grove of ancient live oaks. Printed on the breakfast menu we noticed "The Oaks Prayer for Today."

Slow me down, Lord. Ease the pounding of my heart by the quieting of my mind.... Teach me the art of taking minute vacations: of slowing down to look at seashells, to chat with a friend, to pet a dog.... Let me look up into the towering oaks and know they grew great and strong because they grew slowly and well.

Minute vacations—could I really recapture this kind of stress release in the workaday world? Back home, I experimented. A stretching exercise or two. A stroll around the yard. A few minutes with a crossword puzzle. I developed a score of instant escapes, spending a moment in another time and place.

To stop, to step aside, to lay down the pressure to achieve is to see all the other minutes in a new way, to receive time itself as a daily blessing.

Every now and again
take a good look at something
not made with hands—
a mountain, a star, the turn of a stream.
There will come to you
wisdom and patience and solace and,
above all, the assurance that you
are not alone in the world.

SIDNEY LOVETT

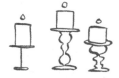

END OF THE DAY REFLECTIONS

At the end of every day—good or bad—
taking time to reflect on the positive can bring to
surface a good memory or two. Keep a
simple joys journal or just make a habit of counting
the blessing of simple things like...

The water fountain worked without shooting water up anyone's nose.
Joey's shoes stayed tied all day.
The pencil sharpener wasn't the main attraction for once.
The rain came after recess.
Lizzy kept her ponytail holder to herself.
Everyone had a lunch today.
Jasmine's sarcasm was blessedly absent.
The butterflies started to hatch.
Juan raised his hand during math.
Nate discovered deodorant.

The reflective life is a way of living that prepares the heart
so that something of eternal significance can
be planted there. Who knows what seeds may come to us,
or what harvest will come of them.

KEN GIRE

*The reflection on a day well spent furnishes us
with joys more pleasing than ten thousand triumphs.*

THOMAS À KEMPIS

Let the one who is wise heed these things and
ponder the loving deeds of the Lord.

PSALM 107:43 NIV

"Elizamath"

BY ANDREW ATTAWAY

Lead me in Your truth, and teach me,
for You are the God of my salvation.

PSALM 25:5 NKJV

This past year our daughter Elizabeth's obsession was numbers. Our nightly game was a pretend circus; in the center ring, the one, the only "Elizamath." At bedtime it was "number stories." No cuddly animals, no shining knights. Just numbers.

"Once upon a time, there was a number sixty-four. He lived in a big house in a little forest, and he was very lonely. So he went to the King of Numbers and asked for some friends. 'Well,' said the king, 'I have some very nice sixteens here. Would you like to adopt them?' 'Oh, yes, please!' said the sixty-four, and he took the sixteens home with him.

"When he got home, he had the sixteens stand one on top of the other. And they were exactly the same height as the sixty-four! How many sixteens were there?"

Elizabeth began to jump up and down on the bed with excitement. "Four! Four!" she shouted.

Elizabeth enjoys solving math problems because their answers are either true or false. When she's right, she knows she's right—there's no uncertainty here. I hope that simple joy in knowing the right answer will follow her throughout her life. And when she's older, and grappling with problems more difficult than arithmetic, I hope that her desire for truth will keep her faithful to Him who is Truth itself, and that she will know God's goodness and glory with the same assurance and enthusiasm as the times tables she learned as a child.

Why did God give us imaginations? Because they help unfold His kingdom. Imagination unveils the Great Imaginer. In the beginning, God created. He imagined the world into being. Every flower, animal, mountain, and raibow is a product of God's creative imagination.

JILL M. RICHARDSON

HOMEWORK JOKES

Q. Why is 2+2=5 like your left foot?
A. It's not right.

Q. What do you do if a student rolls his eyes at you?
A. Pick them up and roll them back!

Q. What happened when the teacher tied all the kids shoe laces together?
A. They had a class trip!

Q. What did the student say to the math worksheet?
A. I'm not a therapist, solve your own problems!

I NEED A BREAK!

We all need a break sometimes—students and teachers. Try out these little de-stressers yourself or as part of your classroom calming routine.

Self Inflate:
Draw in a deep breath, fully expanding your diaphragm. Hold for the count of five and exhale. Repeat as needed. This is a great quick release, perfect for when you're in the middle of a tough moment.

Present Tense:
Great for the end of the day at home, or to help students relax before a test. Can be done standing or lying on the floor (a yoga mat is great for this). Starting with the toes, tense your muscles and keep them tense in this order: toes, foot, ankles, calves, thighs, hips, stomach, chest, shoulders/neck, biceps, elbows, wrists, fingers. Hold for ten seconds and slowly release in backward order.

Mini-Vacation:
Plan a virtual trip to your favorite place. Take five minutes to visualize every detail. Include sights, smells, sounds—the wind in your hair, the sand between your toes, etc. You can go on your own mini-vacation while your students are changing classes or out to lunch.

Honor Roll

A master can tell you what
he expects of you.
A teacher, though, awakens
your own expectations.

PATRICIA NEAL

CHAPTER 5

The simple joy of Encouragement

One of the greatest gifts you can give your children
is your positive expectation of them.

THOMAS HALLER & CHICK MOORMAN

Let everything you say be good and helpful,
so that your words will be an
encouragement to those who hear them.

EPHESIANS 4:29 NLT

Little Hands, Little Feet

BY MARGARET D. DOWNS

Are your hearts tender and compassionate?
Then make me truly happy by agreeing
wholeheartedly with each other, loving one another,
and working together with one mind and purpose.

PHILIPPIANS 2:1–2 NLT

I used to teach school regularly, but multiple sclerosis has reduced my walk to a wobble and my vision is on-again, off-again. I'm now, when able, a substitute teacher. And what wonderful antidepressants those students can be.

For instance, recently I was asked to sub for a kindergarten teacher. I'd been with this class before and always tried to find ways to please their whims. I knew they were expecting something special from me.

As it happened, I'd given them their lessons and had too much time left over. What to do? Quickly I sketched a long, fuzzy caterpillar on the board and asked, "Who can tie his shoes?"

"I can! I can!" came a chorus of raised hands, and I drew a pair of feet on the caterpillar for each child who showed me how they tied their shoes.

Then a small voice piped up, "It's your turn, Teacher. Can you tie your shoes?"

As I bent down, my coordination suddenly deserted me. Embarrassed, I sat there, tears running down my cheeks. *Oh, Father,* I prayed silently, *help me.*

Somehow, the children understood my problem. Within minutes twenty-eight pairs of hands were tying my shoes for me. And so Mr. Caterpillar got another pair of feet. And Teacher thanked God for the helpers that had made her day special.

My Terrible, Horrible, No Good, Very Bad Day

BY MERRY LEE KRAFT

Praise be to...the God of all comfort, who comforts us in all our troubles, so that we can comfort those in any trouble with the comfort we ourselves receive from God.

2 CORINTHIANS 1:3–4 NIV

It was the kind of morning that made me want to hide my alarm clock and burrow under the blankets. Gray skies and relentless rain. But I had to get up. My students were counting on me. Just as I stepped into the tub the lights flickered. No power! No hot water either. I pulled a yellow sweater out of my closet and headed for the garage. I pushed the button for the garage door opener. Oh, yeah, no electricity. Somehow I managed to prop the door open. By then my wet hair was plastered to my sweater. I'd gotten a shower anyway.

At school I was teaching a lesson when the machine I was trying to use would not cooperate. I improvised while the kids fidgeted. Mercifully, class ended and the kids left the room. I followed them into the hall. This day was turning out to be like the title of that popular kids' book, *Alexander and the Terrible, Horrible, No Good, Very Bad Day.*

Lord, I prayed, *will nothing good happen for me today?* That's when I noticed one of my second graders standing shyly next to me. She handed me a piece of paper decorated with flowers and butterflies. "Dear Mrs. Kraft, I love your class." In the center was a smiling stick figure with long brown hair and a bright yellow sweater. "Thank you, Cassie!" I said, wrapping her in a big hug. Her beautiful, grateful smile was just about the quickest answer to prayer I had ever received.

We find delight in the beauty and happiness of children that makes the heart too big for the body.

RALPH WALDO EMERSON

10 SIMPLE WAYS TO SAY "I CARE"

1. Create a secret word, sign, or gesture of affection for each student—greet them with it as often as possible.
2. Let your students overhear you compliment them to someone else.
3. Make up a special cheer to celebrate everyday accomplishments and simple joys (like no tardies or everyone did their homework).
4. Add an encouraging note to a not-so-perfect assignment pointing out what the student did right.
5. Read to your students—even to the ones who are old enough to read to themselves.
6. Proudly display the gifts your students make for you.
7. Tell stories now and then about your childhood and let them see you as a kid.
8. Remind them of something they've taught you and how much you appreciate it.
9. Teach your students to do something you loved as a child.
10. Don't allow other things to distract you when a student wants to talk. Really listen.

When children seek attention,
affection, encouragement, and
unconditional love, they are
not asking for exorbitant gifts.
These are the staples of their soul.

BARBARA FARMER

Love each other with genuine affection, and
take delight in honoring each other.

ROMANS 12:10 NLT

Who's Encouraging Me?

BY GAIL THORELL SCHILLING

Therefore encourage one another and build each other up.
1 THESSALONIANS 5:11 NIV

I'm taking a break from grading research papers: eight done and thirty-two more to go. Grading each paper takes at least fifteen to twenty minutes, so the "done" stack rises slowly. I still face hours of intense work.

Over the past month, my community college students have invested twenty to thirty hours of their lives in this project. They brainstormed topics, evaluated references, drafted, revised, complained—endlessly—and documented sources. I coaxed them through obstacles like jobs, cranky computers, fussy children, colds and flu to meet their deadlines.

But now I wonder, *Who's encouraging me?* I sink down with a small stack and my purple pen, ready to read. But first I read the students' evaluations of their own papers.

"This turned out to be fascinating," writes one. "I didn't know so much had happened in my hometown."

"The more I read about this, the more I wanted to do something to change it," says another.

"One-on-one with the instructor helped me the most," admits the one who nearly dropped the course. "I didn't know I could write." Wow, I think, I reached him after all.

I sit up straighter, energized by these writers and their newfound confidence. I urged them on for the first fourteen weeks of the semester, and they're supercharging me for the final two.

Encouragement is awesome.
It has the capacity to lift a man's or woman's
shoulders. To spark the flicker of a smile
on the face of a discouraged child. To breathe fresh
fire into the fading embers of a smoldering dream.
To actually change the course of another
human being's day, week, or life.

CHARLES R. SWINDOLL

Get along among yourselves, each of you doing your part....
Gently encourage the stragglers, and reach out for the exhausted, pulling
them to their feet. Be patient with each person, attentive
to individual needs. And be careful that when you get on each other's
nerves you don't snap at each other. Look for the best in
each other, and always do your best to bring it out.

1 THESSALONIANS 5:13–15 MSG

UNITY

from "Thoughts into Poetry" by Cleo V. Swarat

I dreamed I stood
in a studio
And watched two
sculptors there,
The clay they used
was a young child's mind
And they fashioned it with care.

One was a teacher;
the tools she used
were books and
music and art;
One was a parent
with a guiding hand
and a gentle loving heart.

And when at last
their work was done
They were proud of
what they had wrought
For the things they
had worked into the child
Could never be
sold or bought.

And each agreed she
would have failed
if she had worked alone
For behind the parent
stood the school,
and behind the teacher
stood the home.

TEACHERS ARE GOOD AT...

making reading fun
never giving up on anybody
believing in miracles
showing and teaching respect
striving for excellence, not perfection
being brave
smiling a lot
never depriving children of hope
being tough minded but tender hearted
showing enthusiasm even when they don't feel like it
keeping promises
creative solutions
avoiding the negative and seeking the positive
listening
doing more than is expected
being a friend
sharing
forgiving
having a good sense of humor
being a dream maker
giving their heart
making a difference

PASSING NOTES

It's often frowned upon to pass notes in class, but not if the teacher is passing them! Give your students or fellow teachers the gift of encouragement by slipping them a note that lifts them up and sends them positively on their way.

Don't know what to say? Try these note starters:

- You always put a smile on my face when you...
- Thanks for the great example in class today...
- I'm so proud of you taking on that homework challenge...
- Thanks for your help in cleaning up and making it fun...
- What a nice thing you did today for...
- I'm impressed! That was a tough thing to do but you did it anyway...
- You make me want to be a better teacher when you…

Honor Roll

What nobler employment,
or more valuable to the state,
than that of the man who
instructs the rising generation.

MARCUS TULLIUS CICERO

CHAPTER 6

The simple joy of Leading

A young child, a fresh, uncluttered mind,
a world before him—
to what treasures will you lead him?

GLADYS M. HUNT

*My goal is that they may be encouraged in heart and united in love,
so that they may have the full riches of complete understanding,
in order that they may know the mystery of God, namely, Christ, in
whom are hidden all the treasures of wisdom and knowledge.*

COLOSSIANS 2:2–3 NIV

My Old School (Bus)

BY EDWARD GRINNAN

Pay attention and turn your ear to the sayings of the wise.

PROVERBS 22:17 NIV

*Y*ellow is the color of September. Why yellow? School busses. This is when they emerge from their summer hibernation to perform the most basic requirement of education—getting kids to school.

You learn a lot on a school bus. Like what other kids have for lunch and the inner-workings of the social networks. You learn about the limits of adult patience in the person of the driver who has to keep one eye on the kids and both eyes on the road.

My driver was a fellow named Mel, who was as important to my education as any teacher. I was a safety boy, which meant I was Mel's enforcer on the bus. It was my first taste of power. Mel noticed I was a little lax when it came to applying the rules to my friends and taught me that the first rule of being respected is to be fair. He also taught me about authority: "Don't be an instigator, Eddie; be a peacemaker."

And the summer I got hit by a car on my bike and spent most of August in traction, it was Mel who visited every week and cried the first time he saw me all banged up.

I like to think about all those bus drivers who are often the vanguard of our educational system. They remind me of old Mel, and all the wise and wonderful people God has put on my road in life.

The potential possibilities of any child are the most intriguing and stimulating in all creation.

RAY L. WILBUR

THE SIMPLE JOY OF CHOCOLATE!

Give yourself a treat—or treat the whole class—with these quick and easy recipes.

Cookie Brownies

Chocolate chip cookies are hard to beat, but scooping out the individual cookie-size dough can be time consuming. To save time, try the pan variation on the back of the chocolate chip bag. Make the dough as usual but spread it into a 9 x 13 pan, bake for 20–25 minutes or until golden brown. Cut into bars and enjoy!

PB and the Chips

Make sandwiches out of Ritz® crackers and peanut butter. Toss some chocolate chips into the peanut butter, and—voilá!—a satisfying snack.

Chocolate Haystacks

Melt 1 cup semisweet chocolate chips with 1 tablespoon butter in a large microwave-safe bowl for 1 minute at medium power in the microwave. Stir, repeat if necessary, until chocolate is melted. Add one small bag of chow mein noodles to mixture and stir until well coated. Drop a tablespoonful onto a waxed paper-lined baking sheet. Chill for 1 hour or until firm. Yum!

Life is no brief candle to me. It is a...splendid torch...
and I want to make it burn as brightly as possible before
handing it over to future generations.

GEORGE BERNARD SHAW

This I learned from the shadow of a tree,
That to and fro did sway against a wall,
Our shadow selves, our influence, may fall
Where we ourselves can never be.

ANNA HAMILTON

Lord, help me do great things as though they were little,
since I do them with Your powers; and help me to do little things as
though they were great, because I do them in Your name.

BLAISE PASCAL

Writing Is Not Enough

BY SHARON FOSTER

Then people brought little children
to Jesus for him to place his hands
on them and pray for them.

MATTHEW 19:13 NIV

I've been known to visit the high school to meet with students for an hour or two, but now I've committed myself to work for two months with a specific group of kids. The school has a bad reputation and its academic scores are probably the worst in the city. But when I walk through the heavy metal doors, pass the metal detectors, and see the smiling faces, I realize that they are children just like mine and each one is like the child I used to be.

They are a little shy at first and sit in their separate cliques, but like a mother hen I gather them all together. They are different nationalities, but soon we are one big family. My plan is not to teach but to listen; I want to give them a place where they can say what's on their minds and where they will learn to respect one another. By the second week they are asking, "Can we start writing now, Miss Foster?"

They tell me stories of broken homes, family arguments, abuse, and immigration. They find the courage, even the shy ones, to read their stories out loud. They encourage each other, tease each other, and support each other. They read things so emotionally honest that I want to cry.

Writing is not enough, I think, so when I'm away from them I pray: *Lord, bless all the children of the world and help us to remember that they belong to Your family and to our families as well.*

Don't follow the path. Go where there is no path
and begin the trail. When you start a new trail equipped with courage,
strength, and conviction, the only thing that can stop you is you!

RUBY BRIDGES

Never tell people how to do things. Tell them what to do,
and they will surprise you with their ingenuity.

GEORGE S. PATTON JR.

That energy which makes a child
hard to manage is the energy which afterward
makes him a manager of life.

HENRY WARD BEECHER

The people who build the future are those who know
that greater things are yet to come, and
that they themselves will help bring them about.

MELVIN J. EVANS

You are not here merely to make a living.
You are here in order to enable the world to live
more amply, with greater vision, with a
finer spirit of hope and achievement. You are here
to enrich the world, and you impoverish
yourself if you forget the errand.

WOODROW WILSON

*What you are becoming is more
important than what you are accomplishing.*

Love and truth form a good leader;
sound leadership is founded on loving integrity.

PROVERBS 20:28 MSG

Inside Out

BY JEFF JAPINGA

The LORD does not look at the things people look at.
People look at the outward appearance,
but the LORD looks at the heart.

1 SAMUEL 16:7 NIV

In our household I'm the go-to guy on laundry day. And, truth be told, I'm pretty much a wiz. Grass stains? Can do. Mud, lasagna (how does a teenager get lasagna on the back of a T-shirt?), no problem. There's only one thing about the laundry that week-in, week-out would send me around the bend: clothes coming out of the dryer inside out.

No big deal, you say? For whatever reason, it was to me. Until I went back to school. Not laundry school but third grade. A teacher-friend of mine had invited me to visit her classroom whenever I wanted. Curious George that I am, I dropped in unannounced one day. Frankly, the room looked like every third-grade classroom with one notable exception: All the children had their clothes on inside out. Shirts, pants, caps—I didn't ask about their underwear! But I did ask what was going on.

Here's what one of the students told me: occasionally, they wear their clothes inside out to remind themselves that with people it's what's on the inside that counts the most.

You won't find me at work today with my clothes reversed, but every time I do the laundry now and clothes come out of the dryer inside out, I don't grumble. I remember it's what's on the inside that counts most.

Sometimes mistakes are the best thing that can happen, because they might lift you out of your lethargy, out of your complacency, and open your mind up to a whole other area that you wouldn't have gone to intentionally.

BOBBY MCFERRIN

Awakening

FROM *THE STORY OF MY LIFE* BY HELEN KELLER

Have you ever been at sea in a dense fog, when it seemed as if a tangible white darkness shut you in, and the great ship, tense and anxious, groped her way toward the shore with plummet and sounding-line, and you waited with beating heart for something to happen? I was like that ship before my education began, only I was without compass or sounding-line, and had no way of knowing how near the harbor was. "Light! give me light!" was the wordless cry of my soul, and the light of love shone on me in that very hour.

I felt approaching footsteps. I stretched out my hand as I supposed to my mother. Someone took it, and I was caught up and held close in the arms of her who had come to reveal all things to me, and, more than all things else, to love me....

We walked down the path to the well-house...and my teacher placed my hand under the spout. As the cool stream gushed over one hand she spelled into the other the word *water*, first slowly, then rapidly.... Suddenly I felt a misty consciousness as of something forgotten—a thrill of returning thought; and somehow the mystery of language was revealed to me. I knew then that "w-a-t-e-r" meant the wonderful cool something that was flowing over my hand. That living word awakened my soul, gave it light, hope, joy, set it free!...

I learned a great many new words that day. I do not remember what they all were; but I do know that *mother, father, sister, teacher* were among them—words that were to make the world blossom for me.

Honor Roll

The dream begins, most of the time,
with a teacher who believes in you,
who tugs and pushes and leads you on to
the next plateau, sometimes poking
you with a sharp stick called truth.

DAN RATHER

CHAPTER 7

The simple joy of Inspiration

You can teach a student a lesson for a day;
but if you can teach him to learn by creating curiosity, he will
continue the learning process as long as he lives.

CLAY P. BEDFORD

The whole earth is filled with awe at your wonders;
where morning dawns, where evening fades,
you call forth songs of joy.

PSALM 65:8 NIV

Inspired Instruction

BY ROBERTA MESSNER

I will instruct you and teach you in the way you should go.

PSALM 32:8 NIV

This past year when I addressed a women's group, I met a lovely lady named Vivian. She explained that my mother had been her first-grade teacher back in the 1940s. "She changed my destination," Vivian said. "Our town was economically challenged, but your mother told us we could change everything through the power of education. I remember running home from school one afternoon to tell my mother, 'We're not poor! My teacher said the whole world is mine because I'm learning to read!'"

From as far back as I can remember, Mother taught me about the joys and rewards of reading. We didn't have much when I was growing up, but thanks to books, we had everything. A poem I saw embroidered on a pillow recently describes my childhood perfectly: "Richer than I, you will never be. For I had a mother who read to me."

I bought some books recently to donate to a local literacy program. It's one more way I'm learning to say a second thank-you for a mother and a teacher who taught me one of the great secrets of the universe.

What we feel, think, and do this moment influences
both our present and the future in ways we may never know.
Begin. Start right where you are.
Consider your possibilities and find inspiration...
to add more meaning and zest to your life.

ALEXANDRA STODDARD

If you want to build a ship,
don't herd people together to collect wood
and don't assign them tasks and work,
but rather teach them to long for the
endless immensity of the sea.

When I approach a child, he inspires in me two sentiments:
tenderness for what he is, and respect for what he may become.

LOUIS PASTEUR

WONDERFUL TEACHER

With a special gift for learning
And with a heart that deeply cares,
You add a lot of love
To everything you share.
And even though you mean a lot,
You'll never know how much,
For you helped to change the world
Through every life you touched.

You sparked the creativity
In the students whom you taught,
And helped them strive for goals
That could not be bought,
You are such a special teacher
That no words can truly tell
However much you're valued
For the work you do so well.

AN INSPIRATION

BY BESSIE ANDERSON STANLEY

He has achieved success who has lived well,
laughed often, and loved much;
Who has enjoyed the trust of women,
the respect of intelligent men,
and the love of little children;
Who has filled his niche and accomplished his task;
Who has never lacked appreciation
of Earth's beauty or failed to express it;
Who has left the world better than he found it,
Whether an improved poppy,
a perfect poem, or a rescued soul;
Who has always looked for the best in others
and given them the best he had;
Whose life was an inspiration;
Whose memory a benediction.

What Makes You Come Alive?

BY PABLO DIAZ

The LORD will work out his plans for my life.

PSALM 138:8 NLT

I ran into Denise, a former coworker who had recently made a career change from technology to teaching. I asked her how things were going. Denise's face lit up and she enthusiastically shared: "I'm teaching seventh grade in a New York City public school in a low-income community. I love it. I am getting up at 4:00 a.m. and getting to bed late, but I feel excited about my job."

Her mission to teach and help inner-city children get an education that would allow them to rise above poverty resonated with me. I was once one of those kids. I knew firsthand the power and positive influence of having a competent and caring teacher in my life. I told her how Mrs. Kelly, my seventh-grade teacher, had a profound impact upon my education. She encouraged me to excel in my school work so I said to Denise, "You will always be remembered by your kids. Teachers live forever in our memories, especially the ones who make an impact upon us."

While Denise continued on her way to the library on a mission, I recalled what a pastor told me when I was young: "Do what makes you come alive." It is exciting to know that God has called each of us to a mission greater than ourselves that makes us come alive.

Think excitement, talk excitement, act out excitement, and you are bound to become an excited person. Life will take on a new zest, deeper interest, and greater meaning. You can think, talk, and act yourself into dullness or into monotony or into unhappiness. By the same process you can build up inspiration, excitement, and a surging depth of joy.

DR. NORMAN VINCENT PEALE

If You Can Quit, I Can Quit

BY GAIL THORELL SCHILLING

And a little child shall lead them.

ISAIAH 11:6 NKJV

I slumped at the kitchen table fighting back tears. The hieroglyphics in my college math book made absolutely no sense. How could I ever become a teacher if I couldn't even learn?

Just then my son Greg burst through the front door. "Yo, Mom! What's up?" I explained that I just couldn't figure out this math problem, fully expecting his sympathy. Greg had always wrestled with schoolwork and never pretended to like junior high. Instead, he grabbed a pencil and said, "Here, do it like this." I compared the answer in the back of the book with his computation and stared at him in respectful amazement. He was right! I couldn't even match wits with a twelve-year-old!

"That does it!" I growled in a fit of self-loathing. "I'm quitting school!"

Greg stopped clowning and said very solemnly, "You can do it, Mom. I know you can. Besides," he looked at me levelly, "if you can quit, I can quit." The challenge was on.

Well, I didn't quit school. By studying and asking my professor regularly for help, I slogged through those frustrating math courses and earned respectable Bs. And now that I'm a teacher, I'm a lot more understanding of students who can't catch a concept the first time around.

When you are inspired by a dream,
God has hit the ball into your court.
Now you have to hit it back with commitment.

DR. ROBERT SCHULLER

This bright, new day, complete with
24 hours of opportunities, choices,
and attitudes comes with a perfectly matched
set of 1,440 minutes. This unique gift,
this one day, cannot be exchanged, replaced,
or refunded. Handle with care.
Make the most of it.
There is only one to a customer!

You Are a Marvel

BY PABLO CASALS

Thank you for making me so wonderfully complex!
Your workmanship is marvelous—how well I know it.

PSALM 139:14 NLT

*E*ach second we live is a new and unique moment of the universe, a moment that will never be again.... And what do we teach our children? We teach them that two and two make four, and that Paris is the capital of France.

When will we also teach them what they are?

We should say to each of them:

Do you know what you are? You are a marvel. You are unique. In all the years that have passed, there has never been another child like you. Your legs, your arms, your clever fingers, the way you move. You may become a Shakespeare, a Michelangelo, a Beethoven. You have the capacity for anything. Yes, you are a marvel. And when you grow up, can you then harm another who is, like you, a marvel?

You must work—we must all work—to make the world worthy of its children.

A word of praise is a "verbal trophy," and
every child has abundant shelf space for such honors.

DR. JAN

*It is not so much what is
poured into the student, but what is
planted that really counts.*

Children live up to what you believe of them.

I will praise You, for I am fearfully and wonderfully made;
Marvelous are Your works, and that my soul knows very well.

PSALM 139:14 NKJV

Honor Roll

Those who can, do.
Those who believe others can also, teach.

JOHN E. KING

CHAPTER 8

The simple joy of Humor

In my belief, you cannot deal with the most serious
things in the world unless
you also understand the most amusing.

WINSTON CHURCHILL

A cheerful heart is good medicine.

PROVERBS 17:22 NIV

Dear Teacher

BY MILDRED B. DUNCAN

What a pleasure to have children who are wise.

PROVERBS 23:24 NLT

Dear Teacher:

Please find attached to this note one six-year-old boy, much cleaner and quieter than usual and with a new haircut and jeans. With him go the prayers of his mother and father.

He's good at creating airplanes and chaos; very adept at tying knots and attracting stray dogs. He especially likes peanut butter, horses, TV westerns, empty boxes, and his shirttail out.

He is allergic to baths, bedtime, taking out the trash, and coming the first time he's called.

He needs to be taught and disciplined, loved and disciplined some more, and reminded to blow his nose and come straight home from school.

After having him in your class and on your nerves, you may not be the same. But I believe you'll be glad to know him because while he tosses books, toys, and clothes, he has a special way of scattering happiness.

Written, I'm afraid with prejudice,
His Mother

When you are dealing with a child,
keep all your wits about you,
and sit on the floor.

A. O'MALLEY

She is clothed with strength and dignity;
she can laugh at the days to come.

PROVERBS 31:25 NIV

A keen sense of humor helps us to overlook
the unbecoming, understand the unconventional,
tolerate the unpleasant, overcome the
unexpected, and outlast the unbearable.

BILLY GRAHAM

People will believe anything if you whisper it.

THE FARMERS' ALMANAC

It now costs more to amuse a child than
it once did to educate his father.

H. V. PROCHNOW

Children are unpredictable.
You never know what inconsistency
they're going to catch you in next.

FRANKLIN P. JONES

*You know children
are growing up when they
start asking questions
that have answers.*

J. J. PLOMP

A cheerful heart has a continual feast.

PROVERBS 15:15 NASB

That Is the Question

BY DANIEL SCHANTZ

The lips of the godly speak helpful words.

PROVERBS 10:32 NLT

*I*t matters how you say something. William Shakespeare said, "To be or not to be, that is the question." That has a certain panache to it, even after all these years. But my college students would say it like this: "So, like, do I want to go on with this gig, or am I, like, outta here? You know what I'm sayin'?" Somehow it's not the same.

Dylan Thomas said, "Do not go gentle into that good night." My students would say, "When my number's up, I'm gonna go kicking and screaming, man."

John Donne wrote, "Never send to know for whom the bell tolls; it tolls for thee." My students would render that, "Yo, dude, sorry I'm late for class. When my alarm went off, I thought it was my roomie's bell."

When I was first married, I wasn't very tactful. I thought the purpose of a disagreement was to win. I would say things like, "Hon, you couldn't be more wrong!" Then I would wonder why the rest of the day didn't go well. After many years of sleeping on the couch,

I learned to say something like, "Hon, you may be right so I'll give your point some more thought." The day goes much better, and I can sleep in our bed.

To be kind or not to be kind, that is the question.

Be kind to unkind people.
It gets to them.

Blessed is he who has learned
to laugh at himself, for he shall never
cease to be entertained.

JOHN BOWELL

THE SIGNS OF A TRUE TEACHER

- You hand a tissue to anyone who sneezes followed by a squirt of hand sanitizer.
- You get more excited about used book sales than shoe sales.
- You move your dinner partner's glass away from the edge of the table.
- The number 100 makes you emotional.
- You ask if anyone needs to go to the bathroom as you enter a theater with a group of friends.
- You see a child being naughty out in public and give them your "teacher stare."
- You hum the "Alphabet Song" as you wash your hands.
- The sight of a lamination machine makes you drool.
- You say everything twice. I mean, you repeat everything.

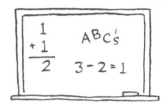

- You have an unhealthy obsession with school supplies.
- You fold your spouse's fingers over the coins as you hand him/her change.
- You're ready to leave school at the end of the day and realize you never did have a chance to use the bathroom.
- You can tell it's a full moon without ever looking outside.
- Every gift you give to your family is educational.
- You encourage your spouse by saying they are a "good helper."
- You have no personal life between Labor Day and Memorial Day.
- You refer to adults as "boys and girls."
- You spend too much time trying to send a text or e-mail with correct spelling and grammar.

Note to Teacher

A note to my daughter's social studies teacher

BY MARK COLLINS

These children are the kingdom's pride and joy.

LUKE 18:16 MSG

Dear Ms. Hoffman,

Please excuse Hope's essay on the Whiskey Rebellion, which did not happen in 1066. Sorry. I told her it did. Age has gnawed away the meat of my memory, leaving tiny crumbs that are ferried about by even tinier ants that struggle to carry things ten times their weight. Anyway, it was the Norman Conquest that happened in 1066. I also remember Norman Lear, Norman Bates, and Norm Cash, who once batted .361 for the Detroit Tigers, in case you're curious.

My brain is now a rucksack of randomness. Then again, some of the arbitrary things I do remember seem worthwhile: my mother reading *Wynken, Blynken, and Nod*. I can almost feel the weight of the three-legged cat that slept on my chest. I remember Hope's first steps—she had footed pajamas, arms like Frankenstein, falling forward into Sandee's lap. I remember as if it were yesterday.

So I admit I can't remember why those crazy folks in my home-town of western Pennsylvania rebelled. But it doesn't mean my memory is faulty, just selective. If I miss a date or two, so be it— as long as it's not a date with my daughter, so I can tell her all about three-legged cats, Frankenstein, and Norm Cash.

Sincerely,
Mr. Collins

Humor is the affectionate communication of insight.

LEO ROSTEN

THE HEART OF A TEACHER

The Fruit of the Spirit

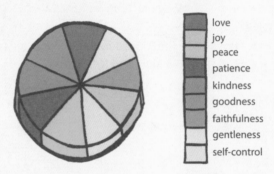

love
joy
peace
patience
kindness
goodness
faithfulness
gentleness
self-control

But what happens when we live God's way? He brings gifts
into our lives, much the same way that fruit appears in an orchard—
things like affection for others, exuberance about life, serenity.
We develop a willingness to stick with things, a sense of compassion
in the heart, and a conviction that a basic holiness permeates
things and people. We find ourselves involved in loyal
commitments, not needing to force our way in life, able
to marshal and direct our energies wisely.

GALATIANS 5:22–23 MSG

THE HEART OF A TEACHER ON A TOUGH DAY

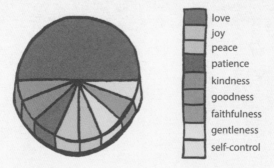

love
joy
peace
patience
kindness
goodness
faithfulness
gentleness
self-control

THE HEART OF A TEACHER ON THE FIRST AND LAST DAY OF SCHOOL

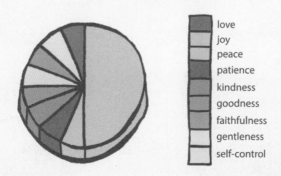

love
joy
peace
patience
kindness
goodness
faithfulness
gentleness
self-control

Honor Roll

One good teacher in a lifetime
may sometimes change a delinquent
into a solid citizen.

PHILIP WYLIE

CHAPTER 9

The simple joy of Sharing

Look deep within yourself and recognize
what brings life and grace into your heart. It is this that can
be shared with those around you. You are loved by God.
This is an inspiration to love.

CHRISTOPHER DE VINCK

*We loved you so much that we shared with you not only
God's Good News but our own lives, too.*

1 THESSALONIANS 2:8 NLT

A Pencil in the Hand of God

BY DANIEL SCHANTZ

You are the ones chosen by God...
God's instruments to do his work and speak out for him.

1 PETER 2:9 MSG

Who could have predicted that a stick of cedar seven inches long would be so useful for so many years to so many people: writers and editors, teachers and test takers, artists and composers, carpenters and puzzle masters?

Perhaps the greatest virtue of the pencil is its abundance. I'm never more than ten feet from a pencil. Almost three billion of them are manufactured every year in America alone.

The pencil is a good metaphor for one of the most treasured of character traits: availability. If I want to be a more valuable and useful person, I need to be more available.

"Can I talk to you for a few minutes; it's important."

"Sure, have a seat."

"Could you give me a hand with these groceries?"

"You bet."

I don't need a college degree, movie-star looks, or money in the bank to be more useful. I just need to be handy. When I say yes, I become a pencil in the hand of God and He can write His story through me.

The most popular technology in my classroom
is an old-fashioned, hand-cranked pencil sharpener.
I have to empty the shavings almost every day.

DANIEL SCHANTZ

Do not forget to do good and
to share with others.

HEBREWS 13:16 NIV

I'm a little pencil in the hands
of a loving God who is writing a
love letter to the world.

MOTHER TERESA

The Big News

BY MELODY BONNETTE

Yes, you should rejoice, and I will share your joy.
PHILIPPIANS 2:18 NLT

When my six-year-old grandson Indy received his first two-wheel bike, the whole family joined in to help him learn to ride it. My daughter Misty, his mom, pushed the bike along; Indy teetered a bit while she coached him on how to balance it. His dad, his younger brothers, and my husband, Johnny, and I called out support along the way.

After a few tries Indy suddenly picked up speed and Misty let him go. He was off on his own, pedaling perfectly down our street. "Way to go, Indy!" we all called out as we clapped for him.

Indy made a big wobbly loop and pedaled back toward us, his face flushed with excitement. He stopped quickly, turned to his mom, and said, "I have to call Miss Westover!"

Indy ran inside to make his phone call, and I followed along. "Hello, Miss Westover? This is Indy Nebeker. I wanted to tell you that I just learned how to ride a two-wheel bike and it only took one hour!" I could hear Miss Westover responding with praise over the phone. Indy beamed with pride. "Bye, Miss Westover."

Indy hadn't asked to call his best friend, his favorite uncle, or his other grandparents. The first person Indy wanted to share his big news with was his teacher.

Train up a child in the way he should go,
Even when he is old he will not depart from it.

PROVERBS 22:6 NASB

Love ever gives—
Forgives—outlives—
And ever stands
With open hands.
And while it lives,
It gives.
For this is Love's prerogative—
To give, and give, and give.

JOHN OXENHAM

SIMPLE GIFTS TO SHARE

The happiness of life is made up of little things—
a **smile**, a **hug**, a moment of shared **laughter**.

Anything, everything, little or big, becomes an
adventure when the right person shares it.

KATHLEEN NORRIS

Happiness seems made to be shared.

JEAN RACINE

Faith is like a boomerang; begin using what you have
and it comes back to you in greater measure.

CHARLES L. ALLEN

The greatest gift is a portion of **yourself**.

RALPH WALDO EMERSON

Be happy with what you have and are,
be **generous** with both,
and you won't have to hunt for happiness.

WILLIAM E. GLADSTONE

BUT I CAN SHARE...

There isn't much that I can do,
but I can share my **bread** with you,
and I can share my **joy** with you,
and sometimes share a **sorrow**, too,
as on our way we go.

There isn't much that I can do,
but I can share my **hopes** with you,
and I can share my **fears** with you,
and sometimes shed some **tears** with you,
as on our way we go.

There isn't much that I can do,
but I can share my **friends** with you,
and I can share my **life** with you,
and oftentimes share a **prayer** with you,
as on our way we go.

Simple Gestures Blossom

BY PAUL BRINKS

The grasslands of the wilderness become a lush pasture,
and the hillsides blossom with joy.

PSALM 65:12 NLT

Leah was surprised when our son, Josh, presented her with a single violet in a little clay pot on Mother's Day. She had decided not to send money with him to kindergarten for the flower sale, since every penny counted in those days. Josh smiled proudly. "Happy Mother's Day!"

Leah later learned that a kind teacher had given Josh some change for the gift. "He was going to spend his milk money on it," the teacher told her. "I knew you wouldn't want him to do that."

Every morning Leah looked at that little clay pot and smiled. In June she and Josh took the single violet outside and planted it in the front yard. Come spring the little violet returned, this time bringing dozens more. A year later those dozens turned into a hundred.

Thirty years later, Josh is a grown man, our finances are secure, and our front yard is filled with violets. Thousands of them. They have never spread into the field behind the house or into any of the neighbors' yards.

On spring mornings I like to look out at that ocean of violets. All from one little flower in a clay pot, bought for the price of a child's carton of milk. Two gestures of love, from a child to his mother and a teacher to a child, and still, all these years later the beauty of it remains. Leah says it's the best Mother's Day present she ever got— a living reminder of what love can do.

*Never underestimate
the influence
of a caring teacher.*

TOP TEN REASONS TO BECOME A TEACHER

10. To "pay it forward"—to be the instigator of future loving, inspiring, and life-changing deeds.

9. To share your passion for learning, for life— for lifelong learning.

8. To see the light of understanding turn on in the eyes of a child—there is no better gift.

7. To be someone's hug—handing out kindness, patience, and understanding to needy hearts.

6. To challenge your creative powers—no two classrooms, two students, or two days are the same in the life of a teacher.

5. To have the opportunity to keep learning for yourself— anyone who keeps learning stays young.

4. To give of yourself in order to see lives grow—
   that is truly living.

3. To get involved in the community—inside and outside
   the classroom, because building relationships with students
   and their families is so rewarding.

2. Recess—there's nothing like a mini-vacation during
   the course of a day to teach others that taking a break is
   healthy and vital.

And the number-one reason to become a teacher:

1. To teach—because you just can't help it!

You are not here merely to make a living.
You are here in order to enable the world to live
more amply, with greater vision,
with a finer spirit of hope and achievement.
You are here to enrich the world.

WOODROW WILSON

Instruct the wise, and they will be even wiser.
Teach the righteous, and they will learn even more.

PROVERBS 9:9 NLT

A child her wayward pencil drew
On margins of her book;
Garlands of flower, dancing elves,
Bud, butterfly, and brook,
Lessons undone, and plum forgot,
Seeking with hand and heart
The teacher whom she learned to love
Before she knew 'twas Art.

LOUISA MAY ALCOTT

Honor Roll

The secret of life is
that all we have and are is a
gift of grace to be shared.

LLOYD JOHN OGILVIE

CHAPTER 10

The simple joy of Faith

There is no greater pleasure than bringing
to the uncluttered, supple mind
of a child the delight of knowing God and the many
rich things He has given us to enjoy.

GLADYS M. HUNT

*Truly I tell you, anyone who will not receive
the kingdom of God like a little child will never enter it.*

LUKE 18:17 NIV

A Moment of Silence

BY ANNE CIBULLA

*Clothe yourselves...with the beauty that comes
from within, the unfading beauty of a gentle
and quiet spirit, which is so precious to God.*

1 PETER 3:4 NLT

*I*t was September 1963. For the first time as an elementary
school teacher I was not to begin the day with a selection
from the Bible and the recitation of the Lord's Prayer. Instead, we
were to observe a moment of silence following the flag salute. I
wondered how a moment of silence could possibly mean anything
to the lively sixth graders I taught.

It was the job of the teacher to explain to the children about
the Supreme Court decision and why the moment of silence had
replaced the Bible reading. "Each of you has the opportunity to
remember God in your own way," I told them. But I wondered if they
really would use the moment in thinking of God.

Days and weeks passed, and I kept wondering if the moment
of silence meant anything to the children. Finally one day, for a
creative writing lesson, I asked my students to share if the moment
of silence had any value to them.

Their answers reassured me: I discovered that it was a very significant part of the school day. Harold Rosenberg's composition was one of many which proved to me that God is not forgotten in my classroom:

"During the moment of silence I pray for world peace and that every person will live very happily. I thank God for letting me live in freedom and in a good clean place. I ask Him to forgive me for all my sins and if I need anything I ask Him for help. I do this not because I have to but because I want to. I think if God made us and takes care of us we can at least thank Him for it."

*Faith, as the Bible defines it,
is present-tense action. Faith means
being sure of what we hope for...now.
It means knowing something is real, this moment,
all around you, even when you
don't see it. Great faith isn't the ability
to believe long and far into the
misty future. It's simply taking God at
His word and taking the next step.*

JONI EARECKSON TADA

The fairest flower in the garden of creation
is a young mind, offering and unfolding itself to
the influence of divine wisdom.

J. E. SMITH

May he give you the power
to accomplish all the good things
your faith prompts you to do.

2 THESSALONIANS 1:11 NLT

Fragile Moments

BY PHYLLIS I. MARTIN

I always thank my God when I pray for you...
because I keep hearing about your faith in the Lord Jesus
and your love for all of God's people.

PHILEMON 1:4–5 NLT

Storm clouds and strong gusts of wind had come up suddenly over Columbus, Ohio. The Alpine Elementary School radio blared tornado warnings. It was too dangerous to send the children home. Instead, they were taken to the basement, where the children huddled together in fear. We teachers were worried too. Child after child began to cry—we could not calm them.

Then a teacher, whose faith seemed equal to any emergency, whispered to the child closest to her, "Aren't you forgetting something, Kathie? There is a power greater than the storm that will protect us. Just say to yourself, 'God is with me now.' Then pass it on to the child next to you."

As the phrase was whispered from child to child, a sense of peace settled over the group. I could hear the wind outside still blowing with the same ferocity of the moment before, but it didn't seem to matter now. Inside, fear subsided and tears faded away. When the all-clear signal came, students and staff returned to their classrooms without their usual jostling and talking.

Through the years I have remembered those calming words. In times of stress and trouble, I have again been able to find release from fear or tension by repeating, "He's with me now."

There is no more significant involvement
in another's life than prevailing, consistent prayer.
It is more helpful than a gift of money,
more encouraging than a strong sermon, more
effective than a compliment,
more reassuring than a physical embrace.

CHARLES SWINDOLL

To grant you health and blessings
And friends to share the way.
I asked for happiness for you
In all things great and small,
But it was His loving care
I prayed for most of all.

Be joyful in hope, patient in affliction, faithful in prayer.

ROMANS 12:12 NIV

DAILY PRAYER

This is a great prayer to recite quietly
while walking to your classroom each day.

I said a prayer for you today
And I know God must have heard,
I felt the answer in my heart
Although He spoke no word.
I asked that He'd be near you
At the start of each new day,
To grant you health and blessings
And friends to share the way.
I asked for happiness for you
In all things great and small,
But it was His loving care
I prayed for most of all.

Gumption

BY D. M.

Do not merely listen to the word.... Do what it says.

JAMES 1:22 NIV

When I was in the seventh grade at North Junior High in Colorado Springs, my home room teacher was Zita Gormley. Undoubtedly, Miss Gormley was an excellent teacher because I enjoyed her classes. But the one thing she taught that I've remembered through the years was not listed in the curriculum. It was "gumption."

Gumption, according to her, was a character trait to be desired, cultivated, and practiced. Gumption made one try harder to excel. Gumption required one to get the assignment done the day *before* it was due. Gumption made one look for the best way, not the easiest way.

Gumption is an action word denoting courage and initiative, enterprise and boldness. It's not lazy and it's not timid.

Sometimes I'm tempted—we all are—to practice a negative kind of piety—avoiding evil by doing nothing. But faith and love demand action. Gumption, if you please. The apostles had it. And if you consider the people you most admire you'll see it being demonstrated in their lives as they teach a Sunday school class, sponsor a youth group, deliver food for "Meals on Wheels," or quietly and tirelessly offer a helping hand where it's needed. Because "doers of the Word" have the gumption to get out of their easy chairs and get into action.

We learn to believe by believing.
We learn to love by loving. The practice
of acting on a certain thing, even
(or especially) when the feeling is absent,
embodies the entire "how" of growth.

EUGENIA PRICE

Honor Roll

The future of the world is in my classroom today....
Only a teacher? Thank God I have a calling
to the greatest profession of all!
I must be vigilant every day, lest I lose
one fragile opportunity to improve tomorrow.

IVAN WELTON FITZWATER

ACKNOWLEDGMENTS

"Bumper Sticker" by Rick Hamlin appeared in *Daily Guideposts*. Copyright © 1980. Used by permission of Guideposts. All rights reserved. Guideposts.org. • "Returning the Favor" by Nancy B. Gibbs appeared in *Guideposts Magazine*. Copyright © 2003. Used by permission of Guideposts. All rights reserved. Guideposts.org. • "Common Denominator" by Z. B. D. appeared in *Daily Guideposts*. Copyright © 1979. Used by permission of Guideposts. All rights reserved. Guideposts.org. • "Beauty for Ashes" by Winifred Waltner appeared in *Guideposts Magazine*. Copyright © 1996. Used by permission of Guideposts. All rights reserved. Guideposts.org. • "Lesson Learned" by B. W. D. appeared in *Daily Guideposts*. Copyright © 1981. Used by permission of Guideposts. All rights reserved. Guideposts.org. • "Finding Wisdom" by Marilyn Morgan King appeared in *Daily Guideposts*. Copyright © 2008. Used by permission of Guideposts. All rights reserved. Guideposts.org. • "How to Punctuate Life" by Sue Monk Kidd appeared in *Guideposts Magazine*. Copyright © 1990. Used by permission of Guideposts. All rights reserved. Guideposts.org. • "Ain't Misbehavin'" by Catherine Scott appeared in *Guideposts Magazine*. Copyright © 2001. Used by permission of Guideposts. All rights reserved. Guideposts.org. • "Mighty Little Note" by Adrian DeGalan appeared in *Guideposts Magazine*. Copyright © 1974. Used by permission of Guideposts. All rights reserved. Guideposts.org. • "When There Is a Need" by Alma Hendrix McNatt appeared in *Guideposts Magazine*. Copyright © 1973. Used by permission of Guideposts. All rights reserved. Guideposts.org. • "A Genius for Loving" by Mary Ann Bird appeared in *Guideposts Magazine*. Copyright © 1984. Used by permission of Guideposts. All rights reserved. Guideposts.org. • "No More Math Problems" by C. A. appeared in *Daily Guideposts*. Copyright © 1980. Used by permission of Guideposts. All rights reserved. Guideposts.org. • "Time Out" by Elizabeth Sherrill appeared in *Daily Guideposts*. Copyright © 2003. Used by permission of Guideposts. All rights reserved. Guideposts.org. • "Elizamath" by Andrew Attaway appeared in *Daily Guideposts*. Copyright © 2001. Used by permission of Guideposts. All rights reserved. Guideposts.org. • "Little Hands, Little Feet" by Margaret D. Downs appeared in *Guideposts Magazine*. Copyright © 1990. Used by permission of Guideposts. All rights reserved. Guideposts.org. • "My Terrible, Horrible, No Good, Very

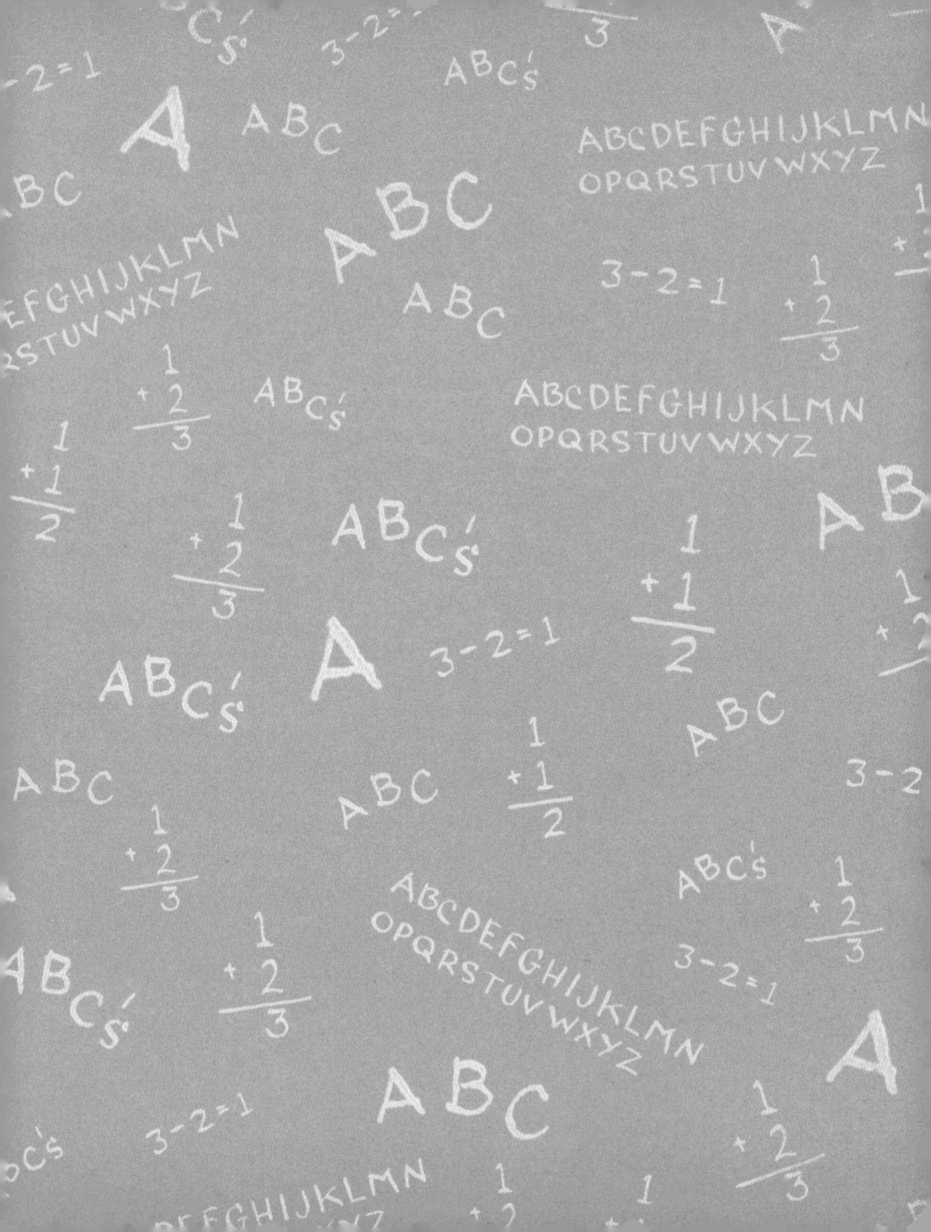

ABC
ABC's
ABCDEFGHIJKLMN
OPQRSTUVWXYZ
3-2=1
1 + 2 = 3
1 + 1 = 2